First World War
and Army of Occupation
War Diary
France, Belgium and Germany

31 DIVISION
Headquarters, Branches and Services
Royal Army Veterinary Corps
Assistant Director Veterinary Services
1 March 1916 - 27 April 1919

WO95/2348/4

The Naval & Military Press Ltd
www.nmarchive.com
Published in association with The National Archives

Published by

The Naval & Military Press Ltd

Unit 10 Ridgewood Industrial Park,

Uckfield, East Sussex,

TN22 5QE England

Tel: +44 (0) 1825 749494

www.naval-military-press.com

www.nmarchive.com

This diary has been reprinted in facsimile from the original. Any imperfections are inevitably reproduced and the quality may fall short of modern type and cartographic standards.

© **Crown Copyright**
Images reproduced by permission of The National Archives, London, England, 2015.

Contents

Document type	Place/Title	Date From	Date To
Heading	WO95/2348-4		
Heading	31st Division Divl Troops Asst Dir. Vety Services Mar 1916-Apl 1919		
War Diary	Post Loud.	01/03/1916	01/03/1916
War Diary	Marseilles.	07/03/1916	07/03/1916
War Diary	Hallencourt.	09/03/1916	27/03/1916
War Diary	Bus Les Artois.	28/03/1916	12/04/1916
War Diary	Bus.	13/04/1916	30/04/1916
Heading	To The Officer i/c Adjutant General Office At The Base. War Diary Bn The Month Of April 1916 Is Forwarded Herewith.		
War Diary	Bus.	01/05/1916	31/05/1916
Heading	D.A.G. G.H.Q. 3rd Echelon Herewith War Diary for June 1916 RI Masseur Major Avc A.D.V.S. 31st Division.		
War Diary	Bus.	01/06/1916	30/06/1916
Heading	War Diary Of A.D.V.S. 31st Div 1st July to 31st July 1916 Vol 5.		
War Diary	Bus.	01/07/1916	06/07/1916
War Diary	Ribeaucourt.	07/07/1916	08/07/1916
War Diary	St Vennant.	09/07/1916	16/07/1916
War Diary	Lestrem.	17/07/1916	31/07/1916
Heading	War Diary of A.D.V.S. 31st Divn Aug 1916 Vol 6.		
War Diary	Lestrem.	01/08/1916	31/08/1916
Heading	War Diary A.D.V.S. 31st Division September 1916 Vol 7.		
War Diary	Lestrem.	01/09/1916	16/09/1916
War Diary	Locon.	17/09/1916	30/09/1916
Heading	War Diary A.D.V.S. 31st Division October 1916 Volume 8.		
War Diary	Locon.	01/10/1916	08/10/1916
War Diary	Marieux.	09/10/1916	16/10/1916
War Diary	Authie.	17/10/1916	31/10/1916
Heading	War Diary A.D.V.S. 31st Division November 1916 Vol 9.		
War Diary	Authie.	01/11/1916	29/11/1916
War Diary	Couin.	30/11/1916	30/11/1916
Heading	War Diary A.D.V.S. 31st Division December 1916 Vol 10.		
War Diary	Couin.	01/12/1916	31/12/1916
Heading	War Diary A.D.V.S. 31st Division January 1917 Vol XI.		
War Diary	Couin.	01/01/1917	10/01/1917
War Diary	Beauval.	11/01/1917	21/01/1917
War Diary	Bernaville.	22/01/1917	31/01/1917
Heading	War Diary. A.D.V.S. 31st Division February 1917 Vol 12.		
War Diary	Bernaville.	01/02/1917	19/02/1917
War Diary	Beauval.	20/02/1917	20/02/1917
War Diary	Authie.	21/02/1917	28/02/1917

Heading	War Diary A.D.V.S. 31st Division March 1917 Volume XV.		
War Diary	Authie.	01/03/1917	03/03/1917
War Diary	Couin.	04/03/1917	19/03/1917
War Diary	Bouquemaison.	20/03/1917	20/03/1917
War Diary	Ramecourt.	21/03/1917	21/03/1917
War Diary	Pernes.	22/03/1917	23/03/1917
War Diary	Norrent Fontes.	24/03/1917	24/03/1917
War Diary	St. Venant.	25/03/1917	31/03/1917
Heading	War Diary A.D.V.S. 31st Division April 1917 Volume XVI.		
War Diary	St. Venant.	01/04/1917	07/04/1917
War Diary	La Pognoy.	08/04/1917	10/04/1917
War Diary	Bruay.	11/04/1917	14/04/1917
War Diary	Ourton.	15/04/1917	29/04/1917
War Diary	Maroeuil.	30/04/1917	30/04/1917
Heading	War Diary A.D.V.S. 31st Division May 1917 Volume XVII.		
War Diary	Maroeuil.	01/05/1917	31/05/1917
Heading	War Diary D.A.D.V.S. 31st Division June 1917 Volume XVIII.		
War Diary	In The Field.	01/06/1917	13/06/1917
War Diary	Maroeuil.	14/06/1917	16/06/1917
War Diary	St Catherine.	17/06/1917	30/06/1917
Heading	War Diary D.A.D.V.S. 31st Division July 1917 Volume XIX.		
War Diary	Field.	01/07/1917	31/07/1917
Heading	War Diary D.A.D.V.S. 31st Division August 1917 Volume XX.		
War Diary	Field.	01/08/1917	31/08/1917
Heading	War Diary D.A.D.V.S. 31st Division September 1917 Volume XXI.		
War Diary	Field.	01/09/1917	30/09/1917
Heading	War Diary D.A.D.V.S. 31st Division October 1917 Volume XII.		
War Diary	Field.	01/10/1917	31/10/1917
Heading	War Diary. D.A.D.V.S. 31st Division November 1917 Volume XXIII.		
War Diary	Field.	01/11/1917	30/11/1917
Heading	War Diary. D.A.D.V.S. 31st Division December 1917 Volume XXIV.		
War Diary	Field.	01/12/1917	28/02/1918
War Diary	Field.	01/02/1918	30/04/1918
Heading	War Diary D.A.D.V.S. 31 Divn May, 1918 Volume XXIX.		
War Diary	Field.	01/05/1918	31/07/1918
War Diary	In The Field.	01/08/1918	16/08/1918
War Diary	Field.	17/08/1918	25/02/1919
War Diary	St Omer.	26/02/1919	30/03/1919
War Diary	Blondecque.	31/03/1919	31/03/1919
War Diary	Blendecques.	01/04/1919	27/04/1919

WD95/2348/4

31ST DIVISION
DIVL TROOPS

ASST DIR. VETY SERVICES
MAR 1916 - APL 1919

Army Form C. 2118.

WAR DIARY
or
INTELLIGENCE SUMMARY.
(Erase heading not required.)

Instructions regarding War Diaries and Intelligence Summaries are contained in F. S. Regs., Part II. and the Staff Manual respectively. Title pages will be prepared in manuscript.

Place	Date	Hour	Summary of Events and Information	Remarks and references to Appendices
Port Said	1.3.16		Embarked on S.S. "Minneapolis"	
	1.3.16 to 6.3.16		At Sea	
Marseilles	7.3.16		Left Marseilles by train for ABBEVILLE	
Pon HALLENCOURT	9.3.16		Arrived at PONT-REMY & marched to HALLENCOURT	
HALLENCOURT	10.3.16		Routine work	
"	11.3.16		Routine work	
"	12.3.16		O/6 motor car available for A.D.V.S.; all cars of Quartermaster were required for other work. This is most unsatisfactory. The D.D.V.S. cannot be properly done without a car	Mar 16 K Mar 19
	13.3.16		Routine work	
	14.3.16		Routine work	
	15.3.16		Routine work	
	16.3.16		Routine work	
	17.3.16		Routine work	
	18.3.16		Saw D.D.V.S. & D.A.D.V.S. & arranged evacuation of two hundred old horses	
	19.3.16		Routine work	

WAR DIARY
or
INTELLIGENCE SUMMARY.

(Erase heading not required.)

Army Form C. 2118.

Place	Date	Hour	Summary of Events and Information	Remarks and references to Appendices
HALLENCOURT	20.3.16		Demonstration to veterinary officers of medium testing in eyelid at 82 Veterinary Hospital ABBEVILLE	
"	21.3.16		Another demonstration at ABBEVILLE 9 reactors shown	
"	22.3.16		Reactors again shown.	
"	23.3.16		Attended conference at DDVS's office	
"	24.3.16		Routine work	
"	25.3.16		Routine work	
"	26.3.16		Routine work	
"	27.3.16		Routine work	
Bns de Arques	28.3.16		Routine work. Moved Hd Bno tes ARTOIS	
"	29.3.16		Routine work	
"	30.3.16		Routine work	
"	31.3.16		Routine work	

Army Form C. 2118.

WAR DIARY
or
INTELLIGENCE SUMMARY.
(Erase heading not required.)

A DVS 31D Vol 2

Place	Date	Hour	Summary of Events and Information	Remarks and references to Appendices
BUS LES ARTOIS	1.4.16		Inspected arm. of 165 Brigade RFA horses with Malone Major Oliver A.V.C. gave a demonstration to our veterinary officers.	
"	2.4.16		Major Oliver A.V.C. came to inspect sick horses. There had moved to new lines & the greatest difficulty was found I much time was lost looking for them.	
"	3.4.16		Inspected arme. arm horses	
"	4.4.16		Inspected Divisional Ammunition Column	
"	5.4.16		Went to ORVILLE to see four horses left by 165" Brigade RFA	
"	6.4.16		Inspected malleined animals. Some of these had been ordered to go to firing line to move guns. Much time lost in finding them	
"	7.4.16		Inspected malleined animals	
"	8.4.16		Inspected malleined animals & reported to D.D.V.S.	
"	9.4.16		Routine work	
"	10.4.16		Routine work	
"	11.4.16		One horse of 171 Brigade reacted malleim & destroyed	
"	12.4.16		Routine work	

Army Form C. 2118.

WAR DIARY
or
INTELLIGENCE SUMMARY.
(Erase heading not required.)

Place	Date	Hour	Summary of Events and Information	Remarks and references to Appendices
B.W.S.	13.4.16		Routine work.	
"	14.4.16		Inspected Divisional Ammunition Column	
"	15.4.16		Routine work	
"	16.4.16		Routine work	
"	17.4.16		Routine work	
"	18.4.16		Routine work	
"	19.4.16		Routine work	
"	20.4.16		Routine work	
"	21.4.16		Routine work	
"	22.4.16		Routine work	
"	23.4.16		Routine work	
"	24.4.16		Routine work	
"	25.4.16		Routine work	
"	26.4.16		Routine work	
"	27.4.16		Routine work	
"	28.4.16		Routine work	

Army Form C. 2118.

WAR DIARY
or
INTELLIGENCE SUMMARY.

(Erase heading not required.)

Instructions regarding War Diaries and Intelligence Summaries are contained in F. S. Regs., Part II. and the Staff Manual respectively. Title pages will be prepared in manuscript.

Place	Date	Hour	Summary of Events and Information	Remarks and references to Appendices
BUS	29/4/15		Newburn 106P/R	
	30/4/15		Newburn 1105/R	

[signature] Major, A.V.C.
A.D.V.S.

To The Officer
i/c Adjutant General's Office
at the Base.

War diary for the month of
April 1916 is forwarded
herewith.

A W Bentley
Col.
ADMS 31st Division

WAR DIARY
or
INTELLIGENCE SUMMARY.

(Erase heading not required.)

Army Form C. 2118.

A.D.V.S. 31st Division Vol 3

Place	Date	Hour	Summary of Events and Information	References to Appendices
H.Q.	1.5.16		Routine work	
"	2.5.16		Routine work	
"	3.5.16		Routine work	
"	4.5.16		Routine work	
"	5.5.16		Routine work	
"	6.5.16		Routine work	
"	7.5.16		Routine work	
"	8.5.16		Application completed and office of A.D.V.S. for 2nd Army	
"	9.5.16		Routine work	
"	10.5.16		Routine work	
"	11.5.16		Routine work	
"	12.5.16		Routine work	
"	13.5.16		Major R.C. Matthews on leave. Capt Banford took over his duties	
"	14.5.16		Lt. Hutchinson admitted to Hospital. Routine work	
"	15-5-16		8th Corps Cavalry Regt attached to this Division for Vety. administration	
"	16.5.16		2 Sections 410 of I Surgeon R.E. and 1 section of Division R.E. attached to this Division	

Army Form C. 2118.

WAR DIARY
or
INTELLIGENCE SUMMARY.
(Erase heading not required.)

Instructions regarding War Diaries and Intelligence Summaries are contained in F.S. Regs., Part II. and the Staff Manual respectively. Title pages will be prepared in manuscript.

Place	Date	Hour	Summary of Events and Information	Remarks and references to Appendices
BUS	17-5-16		Investigated in MAILLY MAILLET a case of suspected poisoning among horses of H Co 191 Bde R.F.A. Result negative.	App B
"	18-5-16		12' Field Ambulance attached to this Division for duty administration	App B
"	19-5-16		2 Section Aux H.S. Ups left the Division	App B
"	20-5-16		Routine work.	App B
"	21-5-16		Routine work	App B
"	22-5-16		Mobile Vety Section moved to THIÈVRES and a collecting post was established at Raincheval	App B
"	23.5.16		Major Matthews A.V.C. returned from leave	App B
"	24.5.16		Took over from Capt Burroughes A.V.C.	App B
"	25.5.16		Routine work	App B
"	26.5.16		Routine work	App B
"	27.5.16		Routine work	App B
"	28.5.16		Routine work	App B
"	29.5.16		Ten cases of spur purning	App B
"	30.5.16		One case spur purning	App B
"	31.5.16		Conference of V. Os Division in case of a forward move.	App B

R.M.Matthews Major A.V.C.
A.D.V.S. 31st Division

Confidential

DAG GHQ
3rd Echelon

Herewith War Diary for June 1916

R Matthews Major AVC
ADVS 31st Division

2/7/16

[Stamp: A.D.V.S. 31st DIVISION No. 2/8.62 Date 2/7/16]

Army Form C. 2118.

Vol 4
June

WAR DIARY
or
INTELLIGENCE SUMMARY.
(Erase heading not required.)

A.D.V.S. 31st Division

Instructions regarding War Diaries and Intelligence
Summaries are contained in F.S. Regs., Part II.
and the Staff Manual respectively. Title pages
will be prepared in manuscript.

Place	Date	Hour	Summary of Events and Information	Remarks and references to Appendices
BUS	1.6.16		Routine work.	R.C.M.
"	2.6.16		Inspected 111 Brigade R.F.A	A.D.M.
"	3.6.16		Inspected Divisional Ammunition Column	A.D.M.
"	4.6.16		Routine work	A.D.M.
"	5.6.16		Inspected 165, 139th R.F.A. & Field Ambulances	A.D.M.
"	6.6.16		Routine work. Inspected 92 Infantry Brigade	A.D.M.
"	7.6.16		Routine work	A.D.M.
"	8.6.16			A.D.M.
"	9.6.16			A.D.M.
"	10.6.16		Went to ABBEVILLE & ordered fans prepared for exchanging	A.D.M.
"	11.6.16		Routine work	A.D.M.
"	12.6.16		One case mange found in 44th Southern Divisional Ammunition Column	A.D.M.
"	13.6.16		Routine work. Inspected 94th 3 Section Div'l Train Col.	A.D.M.
"	14.6.16		Routine work	A.D.M.
"	15.6.16		Routine work	A.D.M.
"	16.6.16		Routine work	A.D.M.

WAR DIARY
or
INTELLIGENCE SUMMARY.   ADVS 31st Division

Army Form C. 2118.

(Erase heading not required.)

Place	Date	Hour	Summary of Events and Information	Remarks and references to Appendices
BDS	17.6.16		Attended conference of VOs of Division at ADMS office	19 CM
"	18.6.16		Attended conference of ADS VS of truck convoy at office of DDVS	19 PM
"	19.6.16		Routine work	19 CM
"	20.6.16		Routine work	19 PM
"	21.6.16		Routine work	19 PM
"	22.6.16		Routine work	19 CM
"	23.6.16		Routine work	19 CM
"	24.6.16		Routine work	19 CM
"	25.6.16		Some operations begun	19 CM
"	25.6.16		Advance post moved to BDS	19 CM
"	26.6.16		Routine work. Very few casualties	19 CM
"	27.6.16		Routine work	19 CM
"	28.6.16		Routine work	19 CM
"	29.6.16		Routine work	19 CM
"	30.6.16		Routine work	

A McMahon Major AVC
ADVS 31 Division

Regimental War Diary
of
ADC 5 31st Divn
1st July to 31st July
1916

WAR DIARY or INTELLIGENCE SUMMARY.

Army Form C. 2118.

(Erase heading not required.)

A.D.V.S. 31st Division

Place	Date	Hour	Summary of Events and Information	Remarks and references to Appendices
BUS	1.7.16		Routine work	ADVM
"	2.7.16		Routine work	RCM
"	3.7.16		Routine work	ACM
"	4.7.16		Routine work	ACM
"	5.7.16		Routine work	ACM
"	6.7.16		Move to RIBEAUCOURT	ACM
RIBEAUCOURT	7.7.16		Routine work	ACM
"	8.7.16		Routine work	ACM
ST VENANT	9.7.16		Move to ST VENANT	ACM
"	10.7.16		Met DDVS 1st Army & arranged inspection of Div Ammn Col	ACM
"	11.7.16		Routine work	ACM
"	12.7.16		D.D.V.S. & DDR First Army inspected Divisional Ammn Col	ACM
"	13.7.16		DDVS & DRR First Army Inspected 165, 169, 170 & 171 Brigades R.F.A.	ACM
"	14.7.16		Routine work	ACM
"	15.7.16		Moved to LESTREM	ACM
"	16.7.16		Arranged trial for Mobile Vety Section	ACM

WAR DIARY
or
INTELLIGENCE SUMMARY.

Army Form C. 2118.

(Erase heading not required.)

A.D.V.S. 31st Division

Place	Date	Hour	Summary of Events and Information	Remarks and references to Appendices
LESTREM	17.7.16		Routine work	R.C.M.
"	18.7.16		Routine work	R.C.M.
"	19.7.16		Routine work	R.C.M.
"	20.7.16		Routine work	R.C.M.
"	21.7.16		Routine work	R.C.M.
"	22.7.16		Routine work	R.C.M.
"	23.7.16		Routine work	R.C.M.
"	24.7.16		Routine work	R.C.M.
"	25.7.16		Inspected 94 Infantry Brigade	R.C.M.
"	26.7.16		Inspected B Battery Brigade RFA. C Battery 305 Brigade RFA. 61st Division that had been in contact with C Battery 305 Brigade RFA. 61st Division that had had a case of glanders.	R.C.M.
"	27.7.16		Routine work	R.C.M.
"	28.7.16		Routine work	R.C.M.
"	29.7.16		Inspected 92 Infantry Brigade	R.C.M.
"	30.7.16		Routine work	R.C.M.
"	31.7.16		Inspected 93rd Infantry Brigade. Conference of V.Os. at this office	R.C.M.

R.C. Matthews Major A.V.C.
A.D.V.S. 31st Division

Confidential

War Diary

of

H.Q. 3rd Army

Aug 1916.

No 11
VOL 6

Army Form C. 2118.

WAR DIARY
or
INTELLIGENCE SUMMARY.   A.D.V.S.

(Erase heading not required.)

Instructions regarding War Diaries and Intelligence
Summaries are contained in F. S. Regs., Part II.
and the Staff Manual respectively. Title pages
will be prepared in manuscript.

Place	Date	Hour	Summary of Events and Information	Remarks and references to Appendices
LESTREM	1.8.16		Inspected 203 & 211 Coys R.E.	ACM
"	2.8.16		Routine work	ACM
"	3.8.16		Routine work	ACM
"	4.8.16		Routine work	ACM
"	5.8.16		Took B Battery 159 Brigade RFA and A Shelter Veterinary conference at DDVS office	ACM
"	6.8.16			ACM
"	7.8.16		DDVS paid army veter supply sectors in 13 & 159 Brigades RFA	ACM
"	8.8.16		Destroyed above horses all now glandered	ACM
"	9.8.16		Routine work	ACM
"	10.8.16		Routine work	ACM
"	11.8.16		Routine work	ACM
"	12.8.16		Routine work	ACM
"	13.8.16		Routine work	ACM
"	14.8.16		Routine work	ACM
"	15.8.16		Routine work	ACM
"	16.8.16		Routine work	ACM

WAR DIARY or INTELLIGENCE SUMMARY.

Army Form C. 2118.

(Erase heading not required.)

ADVS 31st Division

Place	Date	Hour	Summary of Events and Information	Remarks and references to Appendices
LESTREM	17.8.16		Routine work	ADMS
"	18.8.16		Routine work	ADMS
"	19.8.16		Routine work	ADMS
"	20.8.16		Routine work	ADMS
"	21.8.16		Routine work	ADMS
"	22.8.16		Routine work	ADMS
"	23.8.16		Routine work	ADMS
"	24.8.16		Routine work	ADMS
"	25.8.16		Routine work	ADMS
"	26.8.16		Routine work	ADMS
"	27.8.16		Routine work	ADMS
"	28.8.16		Troops inspected on L of C	ADMS
"	29.8.16		Routine work	ADMS
"	30.8.16		Routine work	ADMS
"	31.8.16		Routine work	ADMS

R. Maclean Major AVC
ADVS 31st Division

Confidential   Vol A.Y

War Diary

A.D.V.S.   31st. Division

September 1916.

Army Form C. 2118.

WAR DIARY
or
INTELLIGENCE SUMMARY.
(Erase heading not required.)

A.D.V.S. 51st Division

Instructions regarding War Diaries and Intelligence Summaries are contained in F.S. Regs., Part II. and the Staff Manual respectively. Title pages will be prepared in manuscript.

Place	Date	Hour	Summary of Events and Information	Remarks and references to Appendices
LESTREM	1.9.16		Routine work	ADMS
"	2.9.16		Routine work	ADMS
"	3.9.16		Routine work	ADMS
"	4.9.16		Routine work	ADMS
"	5.9.16		Routine work	ADMS
"	6.9.16		Routine work	ADMS
"	7.9.16		Routine work	ADMS
"	8.9.16		Routine work	ADMS
"	9.9.16		Routine work	ADMS
"	10.9.16		Routine work	ADMS
"	11.9.16		Visited Veterinary Hospital at CALAIS	ADMS
"	12.9.16		Routine work	ADMS
"	13.9.16		Routine work	ADMS
"	14.9.16		Routine work	ADMS
"	15.9.16		Routine work	ADMS
"	16.9.16		Routine work	ADMS

Army Form C. 2118.

WAR DIARY
or
INTELLIGENCE SUMMARY.
(Erase heading not required.)

ADMS 31st Division

Place	Date	Hour	Summary of Events and Information	Remarks and references to Appendices
LOCON	17.9.16		Marched to LOCON	ACM
"	18.9.16		Routine work	ACM
"	19.9.16		Routine work	ACM
"	20.9.16		Conference of V.Os at this office	ACM
"	21.9.16		Routine work	ACM
"	22.9.16		Routine work	ACM
"	23.9.16		Routine work	ACM
"	24.9.16		Routine work	ACM
"	25.9.16		Visit viewing evacuating hospitals at ST OMER	ACM
"	26.9.16		Routine work	ACM
"	27.9.16		Routine work	ACM
"	28.9.16		Routine work	ACM
"	29.9.16		Routine work	ACM
"	30.9.16		Routine work	ACM

A C MacAlmo Major AMC
ADMS 31st Division

"Confidential"

Volume VIII 8

War Diary.

A.D.V.S.

31st Division

October 1916.

Army Form C. 2118.

WAR DIARY
or
INTELLIGENCE SUMMARY.
(Erase heading not required.)

Instructions regarding War Diaries and Intelligence Summaries are contained in F. S. Regs., Part II. and the Staff Manual respectively. Title pages will be prepared in manuscript.

ADVS 31st Division

Place	Date	Hour	Summary of Events and Information	Remarks and references to Appendices
LOCON	1.10.16		Routine work	ACM
"	2.10.16		Routine work	ACM
"	3.10.16		Routine work	ACM
"	4.10.16		Routine work	ACM
"	5.10.16		Routine work	ACM
"	6.10.16		Routine work	ACM
"	7.10.16		Routine work	ACM
"	8.10.16		Moved to MARIEUX	ACM
MARIEUX	9.10.16		Division moving. Some sick men arrived. Great congestion in district	ACM
"	10.10.16		Visited 4th Fd. Amb. Sec. Lieut. FLYNN AVC. arrived for duty	ACM
"	11.10.16		Routine work	ACM
"	12.10.16		Routine work. Capt. J.E. HUTCHINSON. AVC. left division for duty with one no Veterinary Hospital NEUFCHATEL	ACM
"	13.10.16		Routine work	ACM
"			Routine work	ACM

WAR DIARY or INTELLIGENCE SUMMARY

Army Form C. 2118.

Instructions regarding War Diaries and Intelligence Summaries are contained in F.S. Regs., Part II. and the Staff Manual respectively. Title pages will be prepared in manuscript.

A.D.V.S. 31st Division

Place	Date	Hour	Summary of Events and Information	Remarks and references to Appendices
MARIEUX	15.10.16		Routine work	ACM
"	16.10.16		Routine work	ACM
AUTHIE	17.10.16		Moved to AUTHIE	ACM
"	18.10.16		Routine work. Mob Vet Sec moved to AUTHIE	ACM
"	19.10.16		Routine work	ACM
"	20.10.16		Routine work	ACM
"	21.10.16		Routine work	ACM
"	22.10.16		Selected advance post at COIGNEUX	ACM
"	23.10.16		Moved advance post. Place further forward	ACM
"	24.10.16		Routine work	ACM
"	25.10.16		Capt Bamford AVC & Mob Vet Sec went recce. Took over this duties	ACM
"	26.10.16		Routine work	ACM
"	27.10.16		Routine work. Capt Butcher AVC AVP over 41 Mot Vet Sec	ACM
"	28.10.16		Capt Bamford AVC reported evacuated sick	ACM
"	29.10.16		Routine work	ACM
"	30.10.16		Routine work	ACM
"	31.10.16		Routine work	ACM

A.C. Matthews, Major AVC
A.D.V.S. 31st Division

Confidential

Volume XI
W9

War Diary.

A.D.V.S.

31st Division

November 1916.

Army Form C. 2118.

WAR DIARY
or
INTELLIGENCE SUMMARY.

(Erase heading not required.)

Instructions regarding War Diaries and Intelligence Summaries are contained in F. S. Regs., Part II. and the Staff Manual respectively. Title pages will be prepared in manuscript.

A.D.V.S. 31st Division

Place	Date	Hour	Summary of Events and Information	Remarks and references to Appendices
A07 HE	1.11.16		Routine work	ACM
"	2.11.16		Routine work	ACM
"	3.11.16		Routine work	ACM
"	4.11.16		Inspected anything onwards, RA and DVR HQrs Coy	ACM
"	5.11.16		Inspected 93rd Inf. Bgde. Withdrew advance post	ACM
"	6.11.16		Capt. G.H. BUTCHER A.V.C. took over duties of A.D.V.S. during absence of Maj. MATTHEWS on leave to England.	YW. YW.
"	7.11.16		Routine work. Capt. J.M. CROWE A.V.C. reported arrival from England and was posted to 170th Bde R.F.A.	WW.
"	8.11.16		Routine work	WW.
"	9.11.16		D.D.V.S. 5th Army inspected 41st Mob. Vet. Sec.	WW.
"	10.11.16		Routine work.	WW.
"	11.11.16		Routine work. 41st M.V.S.	WW.
"	12.11.16		Routine work. Advanced post re-established at J.16.6.8.3.	WW.
"	13.11.16		Capt. CROWE left for duty with 29th Division.	WW.
"	14.11.16		Capt. BAMFORD reported his arrival.	WW.

Army Form C. 2118.

WAR DIARY
or
INTELLIGENCE SUMMARY.
(Erase heading not required.)

A.D.V.S. 31st Division

Instructions regarding War Diaries and Intelligence Summaries are contained in F. S. Regs., Part II. and the Staff Manual respectively. Title pages will be prepared in manuscript.

Place	Date	Hour	Summary of Events and Information	Remarks and references to Appendices
AUTHIE	15-11-16		Capt Bamford took over duties of OC 41 MVS and ADVS from Capt Butcher who is to report for duty to 170 Bde RFA	Pub B
"	16-11-16		Routine work.	Pub B
"	17-11-16		Major RC Morehuis returned from leave 9 AM OVN	ACM
"	18-11-16		Routine work	ACM
"	19-11-16		Evacuation of animals very heavy at present. Have had to get extra men to assist. Asked Mech Driver sent in a consignment of animals & two men to take them to the Base	ACM
"	20-11-16		Tested mullein 517 Air battery RFA	ACM
"	21-11-16		Tester mullein 517 Her battery RFA	ACM
"	22-11-16		41 Mot Vet Sec on crowded with sick animals. Must it cannot become more	ACM
"	23-11-16		DDVS 4th Army visited 41 Mot Vet Sec	ACM
"	24-11-16		Inspected 165 Bgde RFA wagon lines	ACM
"	25-11-16		Inspected 92 Inf Bgde wagon lines & 95 Field Ambulance	ACM
"	26-11-16		Routine work	ACM

Army Form C. 2118.

WAR DIARY
or
INTELLIGENCE SUMMARY.   A.D.V.S. 31st Division

(Erase heading not required.)

Instructions regarding War Diaries and Intelligence Summaries are contained in F. S. Regs., Part II. and the Staff Manual respectively. Title pages will be prepared in manuscript.

Place	Date	Hour	Summary of Events and Information	Remarks and references to Appendices
AUTHIE	27.11.16		Routine work	ACM
"	28.11.16		Routine work	ACM
"	29.11.16		Routine work	ACM
COUIN	30.11.16		Moved to COUIN	ACM

R Matthews Major AVC
A.D.V.S. 31st Division

Confidential

Volume XII
Vol 10

War Diary.

31st Division

December 1916.

A.D.M.S.

WAR DIARY
or
INTELLIGENCE SUMMARY.
(Erase heading not required.)

Army Form C. 2118.

ADYS. 11th Division

Place	Date	Hour	Summary of Events and Information	Remarks and references to Appendices
GOODIN	1.12.16		Routine work	ACM.
"	2.12.16		Routine work	ACM.
"	3.12.16		Conference D.A.C.	ACM.
"	4.12.16		Conference D.A.C.	ACM.
"	5.12.16		Conference D.T.	ACM.
"	6.12.16		Routine work	ACM.
"	7.12.16		Routine work	ACM.
"	8.12.16		Routine work	ACM.
"	9.12.16		Routine work	ACM.
"	10.12.16		Routine work	ACM.
"	11.12.16		Routine work	ACM.
"	12.12.16		Routine work	ACM.
"	13.12.16		Routine work	ACM.
"	14.12.16		Routine work	ACM.
"	15.12.16		Routine work	ACM.
"	16.12.16		Routine work	ACM.

Army Form C. 2118.

WAR DIARY
or
INTELLIGENCE SUMMARY.

(Erase heading not required.)

ACVS. 31st Division

Instructions regarding War Diaries and Intelligence Summaries are contained in F. S. Regs., Part II. and the Staff Manual respectively. Title pages will be prepared in manuscript.

Place	Date	Hour	Summary of Events and Information	Remarks and references to Appendices
COUIN	17.12.16		Routine work	ACM
"	18.12.16		Routine work	ACM
"	19.12.16		Routine work	ACM
"	20.12.16		Routine work	ACM
"	21.12.16		Routine work	ACM
"	22.12.16		Routine work	ACM
"	23.12.16		Routine work	ACM
"	24.12.16		Routine work	ACM
"	25.12.16		Routine work	ACM
"	26.12.16		Routine work	ACM
"	27.12.16		Routine work	ACM
"	28.12.16		Routine work	ACM
"	29.12.16		Routine work	ACM
"	30.12.16		Routine work	ACM
"	31.12.16		Routine work	ACM

N. Matthews Major A.V.C.
ADVS. 31st Division

Confidential   Volume XIII.

Vol XI

War Diary.

A.D.V.S.   31st Division

January 1917.

Army Form C. 2118.

WAR DIARY
or
INTELLIGENCE SUMMARY.
(Erase heading not required.)

A.D.V.S. 31st Division

Instructions regarding War Diaries and Intelligence Summaries are contained in F. S. Regs., Part II. and the Staff Manual respectively. Title pages will be prepared in manuscript.

Place	Date	Hour	Summary of Events and Information	Remarks and references to Appendices
COUIN	1.1.17		Routine work	ACM
"	2.1.17		Routine work	ACM
"	3.1.17		Routine work	ACM
"	4.1.17		Routine work	ACM
"	5.1.17		Routine work	ACM
"	6.1.17		Routine work	ACM
"	7.1.17		Routine work	ACM
"	8.1.17		Routine work	ACM
"	9.1.17		Routine work	ACM
"	10.1.17		Routine work	ACM
BEAUVAL	11.1.17		Moved to BEAUVAL. 41 Mot. Amb. Sec. moved to BEAUVAL	ACM
"	12.1.17		Routine work	ACM
"	13.1.17		Routine work	ACM
"	14.1.17		Routine work	ACM
"	15.1.17		Routine work	ACM
"	16.1.17		Routine work	ACM

WAR DIARY
or
INTELLIGENCE SUMMARY.
(Erase heading not required.)

Army Form C. 2118.

A.D.V.S. 31st Division

Place	Date	Hour	Summary of Events and Information	Remarks and references to Appendices
BEAUVAL	17.1.17		Routine work	RCM
"	18.1.17		Routine work	RCM
"	19.1.17		Routine work	RCM
"	20.1.17		Routine work	RCM
"	21.1.17		Routine work	RCM
"	22.1.17		Moved to BEAUVAL - BERNAVILLE	RCM
BERNAVILLE	22.1.17		Routine work	RCM
"	23.1.17		Routine work	RCM
"	24.1.17		Routine work	RCM
"	25.1.17		Routine work	RCM
"	26.1.17		Routine work	RCM
"	27.1.17		Routine work	RCM
"	28.1.17		Routine work	RCM
"	29.1.17		Routine work	RCM
"	30.1.17		Routine work	RCM
"	31.1.17		Routine work	RCM

RC Matthews Major AVC
ADVS 31st Division

Confidential

Volume XIV

Vol 12

War Diary.

A.D.S. 31st Division

February 1917.

Army Form C. 2118.

WAR DIARY
or
INTELLIGENCE SUMMARY.

(Erase heading not required.)

Instructions regarding War Diaries and Intelligence Summaries are contained in F. S. Regs., Part II. and the Staff Manual respectively. Title pages will be prepared in manuscript.

Place	Date	Hour	Summary of Events and Information	Remarks and references to Appendices
BERNAVILLE	1.2.17		Routine work	ACM
"	2.2.17		Routine work	ACM
"	3.2.17		Routine work	ACM
"	4.2.17		Routine work	ACM
"	5.2.17		Routine work	ACM
"	6.2.17		Routine work	ACM
"	7.2.17		Routine work	ACM
"	8.2.17		Routine work	ACM
"	9.2.17		Routine work	ACM
"	10.2.17		Routine work	ACM
"	11.2.17		Routine work	ACM
"	12.2.17		Routine work	ACM
"	13.2.17		Routine work	ACM
"	14.2.17		Routine work	ACM
"	15.2.17		Routine work	ACM
"	16.2.17		Routine work. Took over Mules for A.D.S and Mobile Section	ACM

J Bakinbradale
Cap J ave

WAR DIARY
or
INTELLIGENCE SUMMARY.

(Erase heading not required.)

Army Form C. 2118.

ADVS — 31st Division

Place	Date	Hour	Summary of Events and Information	Remarks and references to Appendices
BERNAVILLE	17.2.17		Capt. H. Butcher A.V.C. took over duties of A.D.V.S. from Capt. Idle A.V.C.	
"	18.2.17		Routine work	
"	19-2-17		Routine work	
BEAUVAL	20-2-17		Moved to BEAUVAL	
AUTHIE	21-2-17		Moved to AUTHIE	
"	22-2-17		Routine work	
"	23-2-17		Routine work	
"	24-2-17		Routine work	
"	25-2-17		Routine work	
"	26-2-17		Routine work	
"	27-2-17		Routine work	
"	28.2.17		Took over from Capt. G.H. Butcher AVC	

R.C. Matthew
Major AVC

Confidential

Volume XV. Vol/3

War Diary.

A.D.V.S.

31st. Division

March 1917.

WAR DIARY or INTELLIGENCE SUMMARY

Army Form C. 2118.

ADVS 31st Division

Place	Date	Hour	Summary of Events and Information	Remarks and references to Appendices
AUTHIE	1.3.17		Routine work	ACM
"	2.3.17		Routine work	ACM
"	3.3.17		Routine work	ACM
COUIN	4.3.17		Moved to COUIN	ACM
"	5.3.17		Routine work	ACM
"	6.3.17		Routine work	ACM
"	7.3.17		Routine work	ACM
"	8.3.17		Routine work	RCM
"	9.3.17		Routine work. Attended conference of ADVS. at office of DDVS, Fifth Army	ACM
"	10.3.17		Routine work	ACM
"	11.3.17		Routine work	ACM
"	12.3.17		Routine work	ACM
"	13.3.17		Routine work	ACM
"	14.3.17		Routine work	ACM
"	15.3.17		Routine work. Inspection of R.A. animals by DDVS, Fifth Army	ACM
"	16.3.17		Routine work	ACM

WAR DIARY
or
INTELLIGENCE SUMMARY.
(Erase heading not required.)

Army Form C. 2118.

ADVS 31st Division

Place	Date	Hour	Summary of Events and Information	Remarks and references to Appendices
COUIN	17.3.17		Routine work	ACM
"	18.3.17		Routine work	ACM
"	19.3.17/20.3.17		Routine work	ACM
BOUGUEMAISON			Marched to BOUGUEMAISON	ACM
RAMECOURT	21.3.17		Marched to RAMECOURT	ACM
PERNES	22.3.17		Marched to PERNES	ACM
"	23.3.17		Remained at PERNES	ACM
NORRENT FONTES	24.3.17		Marched to NORRENT FONTES	ACM
ST VENANT	25.3.17		Marched to ST VENANT	ACM
"	26.3.17		Routine work	ACM
"	27.3.17		Inspected R.A. animals & reported to DDVS First Army	ACM
"	28.3.17		Routine work	ACM
"	29.3.17		Routine work	ACM
"	30.3.17		Routine work	ACM
"	31.3.17		Routine work	ACM

AC Matthews Major AVC
ADVS. 31st Division

"Confidential" Volume XVI

Vol 14

War Diary.

A.D.S.   31st Division

April 1917

WAR DIARY
or
INTELLIGENCE SUMMARY.

Army Form C. 2118.

A.D.V.S. 31st DIVISION

Place	Date	Hour	Summary of Events and Information	Remarks and references to Appendices
ST. VENANT	1.4.17		Attended conference of A.D.V.S. at office of D.D.V.S. First Army	ACM
"	2.4.17		Routine work	ACM
"	3.4.17		Routine work	ACM
"	4.4.17		Routine work	ACM
"	5.4.17		Routine work	ACM
"	6.4.17		Routine work	ACM
"	7.4.17		Routine work	ACM
LAPUGNOY	8.4.17		Practices at LAPUGNOY	ACM
"	9.4.17		Routine work	ACM
"	10.4.17		Routine work	ACM
BRUAY	11.4.17		Moved to BRUAY	ACM
"	12.4.17		Routine work	ACM
"	13.4.17		Routine work	ACM
"	14.4.17		Routine work	ACM
OURTON	15.4.17		Moved to OURTON	ACM
"	16.4.17		Routine work	ACM

Army Form C. 2118.

WAR DIARY
or
INTELLIGENCE SUMMARY.
(Erase heading not required.)

A.D.V.S. — 31st Division

Place	Date	Hour	Summary of Events and Information	Remarks and references to Appendices
OURTON	17.4.17		Routine work	ACM
"	18.4.17		Routine work	ACM
"	19.4.17		Routine work	ACM
"	20.4.17		Routine work	ACM
"	21.4.17		Routine work	ACM
"	22.4.17		Routine work	ACM
"	23.4.17		Routine work	ACM
"	24.4.17		Routine work	ACM
"	25.4.17		Routine work	ACM
"	26.4.17		Routine work	ACM
"	27.4.17		Routine work	ACM
"	28.4.17		Routine work	ACM
"	29.4.17		Routine work	ACM
MAROEUIL	30.4.17		Marched to MAROEUIL	ACM

A.C.Matthews Major AVC
ADVS 31st Division

Confidential.

Volume XVII.

War Diary.

A.D.V.S.

51st Division

May 1917.

WAR DIARY
or
INTELLIGENCE SUMMARY.

Army Form C. 2118.

ADVS 31st Division

Place	Date	Hour	Summary of Events and Information	Remarks and references to Appendices
MAROEUIL	1.5.17		Routine work	ACM
"	2.5.17		Placed Advanced Post at ST NICOLAS	ACM
"	3.5.17		Routine work	ACM
"	4.5.17		Routine work	ACM
"	5.5.17		Inspected corrals 170 Bde RFA & new OC Rest Camp	ACM
"	6.5.17		Attended conference ADVS at office of DDVS First Army	ACM
"	7.5.17		Routine work	ACM
"	8.5.17		Routine work	ACM
"	9.5.17		Routine work	ACM
"	10.5.17		Routine work	ACM
"	11.5.17		Routine work	ACM
"	12.5.17		Routine work	ACM
"	13.5.17		Withdrew advance post at ST NICHOLAS	ACM
"	14.5.17		Routine work	ACM
"	15.5.17		Routine work	ACM
"	16.5.17		Routine work	ACM

WAR DIARY
or
INTELLIGENCE SUMMARY.

(Erase heading not required.)

Army Form C. 2118.

ADVS 31st Division

Place	Date	Hour	Summary of Events and Information	Remarks and references to Appendices
MARŒUIL	17.5.17		Routine work	NCM
"	18.5.17		Routine work	NCM
"	19.5.17		Routine work	NCM
"	20.5.17		Routine work	RCM
"	21.5.17		Routine work	NCM
"	22.5.17		Routine work	NCM
"	23.5.17		Routine work	NCM
"	24.5.17		Routine work	RCM
"	25.5.17		Routine work	RCM
"	26.5.17		Routine work	RCM
"	27.5.17		Routine work	RCM
"	28.5.17		Routine work	RCM
"	29.5.17		Routine work	RCM
"	30.5.17		Routine work	RCM
"	31.5.17		Routine work	RCM

AC Matthew Major AVC
A.D.V.S. 31st Division

Confidential

Volume XVIII

Vol 16.

War Diary.

D.A.D.V.S. 31st Division

June 1917

WAR DIARY or INTELLIGENCE SUMMARY

Army Form C. 2118.

DADVS 31st Division

Place	Date	Hour	Summary of Events and Information	Remarks and references to Appendices
In the Field	1-6-17		Capt. G. H. BUTCHER A.V.C. resumed duties of A.D.V.S. during absence of Major MATTHEWS A.V.C. on 10 days leave to England	
"	2-6-17		Routine work	
"	3-6-17		Routine work	
"	4-6-17		Routine work	
"	5-6-17		Visited H.Q. 2nd, 165th & 13th R.F.A. to give instructions regarding anti gas shoe appliances & to memorandise the fitting on of same.	
"	6-6-17		Routine work. A/D.D.V.S. interviewed Lt. FLYNN on application for permanent commission	
"	7-6-17		Routine work. Inspected 13 surplus infantry pack animals prior to return to Remount Section at GONNEHEM	
"	8-6-17		Routine work	
"	9-6-17		Routine work	
"	10-6-17		Routine work	
"	11-6-17		Routine work	
"	12.6.17		Major MATTHEWS returned to duty	
"	13.6.17		Routine work	

WAR DIARY or INTELLIGENCE SUMMARY.

Army Form C. 2118.

DADYS 31st Division

Place	Date	Hour	Summary of Events and Information	Remarks and references to Appendices
MAROEUIL	14.6.17		Routine work	ACM
"	15.6.17		Routine work	ACM
"	16.6.17		Routine work	ACM
ST CATHERINE	17.6.17		Moved to ST CATHERINE	ACM
"	18.6.17		Routine work	ACM
"	19.6.17		Routine work	ACM
"	20.6.17		Routine work	ACM
"	21.6.17		Routine work	ACM
"	22.6.17		Routine work	ACM
"	23.6.17		Routine work	ACM
"	24.6.17		Routine work	ACM
"	25.6.17		Routine work	ACM
"	26.6.17		Routine work	ACM
"	27.6.17		Routine work	ACM
"	28.6.17		Routine work	ACM
"	29.6.17		Routine work	ACM
"	30.6.17		Routine work	ACM

AC Muirhead Major AVC
DADVS 31st Division

Confidential

Volume XIX

Vol 17

War Diary.

31st Division

D.A.D.V.S.

July 1917.

Army Form C. 2118.

WAR DIARY
or
INTELLIGENCE SUMMARY.
(Erase heading not required.)

D.A.D.V.S. 31st Division

Instructions regarding War Diaries and Intelligence Summaries are contained in F. S. Regs., Part II. and the Staff Manual respectively. Title pages will be prepared in manuscript.

Place	Date	Hour	Summary of Events and Information	Remarks and references to Appendices
Field	1.7.17		Routine work	RCM
"	2.7.17		Routine work	RCM
"	3.7.17		Routine work	RCM
"	4.7.17		Routine work	RCM
"	5.7.17		Routine work	RCM
"	6.7.17		Routine work	RCM
"	7.7.17		Routine work	RCM
"	8.7.17		Routine work	RCM
"	9.7.17		Routine work	RCM
"	10.7.17		Routine work	RCM
"	11.7.17		A.D.V.S. 13 Corps inspected Divisional Train. He ordered the evacuation of ten animals & the isolation in the Mot Vet Sec of two. He was of opinion that all were suspicious of mange. I did not agree with this. I considered that they should have been left with the unit.	RCM
"	12.7.17		A.D.V.S. 13 Corps inspected Div Amm Column	RCM

2353 Wt. W2514/1454 700,000 5/15 L. D., D. & L. A.D.S.S./Forms/C. 2118.

Army Form C. 2118.

WAR DIARY
or
INTELLIGENCE SUMMARY.
(Erase heading not required.)

DADVS 31st Division

Instructions regarding War Diaries and Intelligence Summaries are contained in F. S. Regs, Part II. and the Staff Manual respectively. Title pages will be prepared in manuscript.

Place	Date	Hour	Summary of Events and Information	Remarks and references to Appendices
Field	13.7.17		Routine work	ACM
"	14.7.17		Attended conference of DADsVS at office of ADVS 13 Corps	ACM
"	15.7.17		Routine work	ACM
"	16.7.17		Routine work	ACM
"	17.7.17		Routine work	ACM
"	18.7.17		Routine work	ACM
"	19.7.17		ADVS 13 Corps inspected 41 Mot Vet Sec	ACM
"	20.7.17		Routine work	ACM
"	21.7.17		ADVS 13 Corps inspected 165 Bde RFA	ACM
"	22.7.17		Routine work	ACM
"	23.7.17		Moved to FORT GEORGE Camp	ACM
"	24.7.17		Routine work	ACM
"	25.7.17		ADVS 13 Corps inspected 93rd Infantry Bde	ACM
"	26.7.17		Routine work	ACM
"	27.7.17		Routine work	ACM
"	28.7.17		ADVS 13th Corps inspected 170 Bde RFA	ACM

Army Form C. 2118.

WAR DIARY
or
INTELLIGENCE SUMMARY.
(Erase heading not required.)

DADVS 31st Division

Instructions regarding War Diaries and Intelligence Summaries are contained in F. S. Regs., Part II. and the Staff Manual respectively. Title pages will be prepared in manuscript.

Place	Date	Hour	Summary of Events and Information	Remarks and references to Appendices
Field	29.7.17		Routine work	AM PM
"	30.7.17		Routine work	AM PM
"	31.7.17		ADVS 13 AA Corps inspected 94th Infantry Bde.	AM PM

RC Matthews Major AVC
DADVS 31st Division

2353 Wt. W2514/1454 700,000 5/15 D. D. & L. A.D.S.S./Forms/C. 2118.

Confidential

Volume XX
Vol 18

War Diary.

D.A.D.S.   31st Division

6 August 1917

Army Form C. 2118.

WAR DIARY
or
INTELLIGENCE SUMMARY.

(Erase heading not required.)

DADVS 31st Division

Place	Date	Hour	Summary of Events and Information	Remarks and references to Appendices
Field	1.8.17		Routine work	ACM
"	2.8.17		Routine work	ACM
"	3.8.17		ADVS 13th Corps inspected 92nd Infantry Bde	ACM
"	4.8.17		Routine work	ACM
"	5.8.17		Routine work	ACM
"	6.8.17		Routine work	ACM
"	7.8.17		Routine work	ACM
"	8.8.17		Routine work	ACM
"	9.8.17		Routine work	ACM
"	10.8.17		Routine work	ACM
"	11.8.17		Routine work	ACM
"	12.8.17		Routine work	ACM
"	13.8.17		Routine work	ACM
"	14.8.17		Routine work	ACM
"	15.8.17		Routine work	ACM
"	16.8.17		Routine work	ACM
"	17.8.17		Routine work	ACM

Army Form C. 2118.

WAR DIARY
or
INTELLIGENCE SUMMARY.

(Erase heading not required.)

D.A.D.V.S.,
31st DIVISION.

Instructions regarding War Diaries and Intelligence Summaries are contained in F. S. Regs., Part II. and the Staff Manual respectively. Title pages will be prepared in manuscript.

DADVS. 31st Division

Place	Date	Hour	Summary of Events and Information	Remarks and references to Appendices
Field	18.8.17		Routine work	ACM
"	19.8.17		Routine work	ACM
"	20.8.17		Routine work	ACM
"	21.8.17		Routine work	ACM
"	22.8.17		Routine work	ACM
"	23.8.17		Routine work	ACM
"	24.8.17		Routine work	ACM
"	25.8.17		Routine work	ACM
"	26.8.17		Routine work	ACM
"	27.8.17		Routine work. Capt Bright AVC reported arch	ACM
"	28.8.17		Routine work	ACM
"	29.8.17		Routine work	ACM
"	30.8.17		Routine work	ACM
"	31.8.17		Routine work	ACM

AC Matthews Major AVC
DADVS 31st Division

Confidential

Volume XXI

Vol 19

War Diary.

D.A.D.V.S.

31st Division

September 1917.

Army Form C. 2118.

WAR DIARY
or
INTELLIGENCE SUMMARY.

(Erase heading not required.)

D.A.D.V.S. 31st Division

Instructions regarding War Diaries and Intelligence Summaries are contained in F.S. Regs., Part II and the Staff Manual respectively. Title pages will be prepared in manuscript.

D.A.D.V.S. 31st DIVISION.

Place	Date	Hour	Summary of Events and Information	Remarks and references to Appendices
Field	1.9.17		One horse evacuated from C/170 Bde RFA reached No 7 Div Hospital. All animals of battery tested with mallein	RCM
"	2.9.17		Syringe broke & all animals could not be tested last night. Half were tested this morning	RCM
"	3.9.17		Routine work	RCM
"	4.9.17		Routine work	RCM
"	5.9.17		Routine work	RCM
"	6.9.17		ADVS 13th Corps inspected A battery 165 Bde RFA	RCM
"	7.9.17		Moved to ROCLINCOURT	RCM
"	8.9.17		Routine work	RCM
"	9.9.17		Routine work	RCM
"	10.9.17		Routine work	RCM
"	11.9.17		Routine work. D.A.D.V.S. proceeded on 10 days leave to England. Capt. A.M. BUTCHER A.V.C. to take over duties of DADVS during his absence	CMB
"	12.9.17		Routine work	CMB
"	13.9.17		Routine work. A.D.V.S. Corps inspected 94th Bde, 13th & 210 Fd Co R.E.	CMB
"	14.9.17		Routine work	CMB

Army Form C. 2118.

WAR DIARY
or
INTELLIGENCE SUMMARY. D.A.D.V.S. 31st Div^n

(Erase heading not required.)

Instructions regarding War Diaries and Intelligence Summaries are contained in F. S. Regs., Part II. and the Staff Manual respectively. Title pages will be prepared in manuscript.

D.A.D.V.S.
31st DIVISION.

Place	Date	Hour	Summary of Events and Information	Remarks and references to Appendices
Field	15-9-17		Routine work	GWB
"	16-9-17		Routine work	GWB
"	17-9-17		Routine work	GWB
"	18-9-17		Routine work	GWB
"	19-9-17		Routine work	GWB
"	20-9-17		Routine work. Inspected 13th Y & L with O.C. Regt.	GWB
"	21-9-17		Routine work.	GWB
"	22.9.17		Major R.C. MATTHEWS, A.V.C. returned from leave & took over duties	RCM
"	23.9.17		Routine work	RCM
"	24.9.17		Routine work	RCM
"	25.9.17		Routine work	RCM
"	26.9.17		Routine work	RCM
"	27.9.17		ADVS XIII Corps inspected 165 Bde R.F.A.	RCM

Army Form C. 2118.

WAR DIARY
or
INTELLIGENCE SUMMARY.
(Erase heading not required.)

DADVS 31st Division

Place	Date	Hour	Summary of Events and Information	Remarks and references to Appendices
Field	28.9.17		Routine work	ACM
"	29.9.17		Routine work	ACM
"	30.9.17		Routine work	ACM
			AC Matthews Major AVC	
			DADVS 31st Division	

Confidential

Volume XII
WA 20

War Diary.

D.A.D.V.S. 31st Division

October 1917.

WAR DIARY or INTELLIGENCE SUMMARY.

(Erase heading not required.)

Army Form C. 2118.

D.A.D.V.S., 31st Division

Place	Date	Hour	Summary of Events and Information	Remarks and references to Appendices
Field	1.10.17		Routine work	ACM
"	2.10.17		Routine work	ACM
"	3.10.17		Routine work	ACM
"	4.10.17		Routine work	ACM
"	5.10.17		Routine work	ACM
"	6.10.17		Routine work	ACM
"	7.10.17		Routine work	ACM
"	8.10.17		Routine work	ACM
"	9.10.17		A conference of V.Os to discuss the question why this division however a large with but it was decided that minor injuries that took to get recorded in five days will not be shown that all cases of Actinomycosis contagious disease are to be shown the rate that of this division is 2.5 per cent which is not high but it appears to be double that of other divisions	
"	10.10.17		Routine work	ACM
"	11.10.17		Routine work	ACM

Army Form C. 2118.

WAR DIARY
or
INTELLIGENCE SUMMARY.

D.A.D.V.S. 31st Division

(Erase heading not required.)

Place	Date	Hour	Summary of Events and Information	Remarks and references to Appendices
Field	12.10.17		Routine work	RCM
"	13.10.17		Routine work	RCM
"	14.10.17		Routine work	RCM
"	15.10.17		Routine work	RCM
"	16.10.17		Routine work	RCM
"	17.10.17		Routine work	RCM
"	18.10.17		Routine work	RCM
"	19.10.17		Routine work	RCM
"	20.10.17		Routine work	RCM
"	21.10.17		Routine work	RCM
"	22.10.17		Routine work	RCM
"	23.10.17		Routine work	RCM
"	24.10.17		Routine work	RCM
"	25.10.17		Routine work	RCM
"	26.10.17		Routine work	RCM
"	27.10.17		Routine work	RCM

Army Form C. 2118.

WAR DIARY
or
INTELLIGENCE SUMMARY.
(Erase heading not required.)

DADVS 31st Division

Instructions regarding War Diaries and Intelligence Summaries are contained in F. S. Regs., Part II. and the Staff Manual respectively. Title pages will be prepared in manuscript.

Place	Date	Hour	Summary of Events and Information	Remarks and references to Appendices
Field	28.10.17		Routine work	Field RCM
"	29.10.17		Routine work	RCM
"	30.10.17		Routine work	RCM
"	31.10.17		Routine work	RCM
			AC Matthew Major D.A.D.V.S. 31st Division	

Confidential

Volume XXIII
Vol 2 # 21

War Diary.

A.D.M.S. 31st Division

November 1917

WAR DIARY
or
INTELLIGENCE SUMMARY

D.A.D.V.S. 31st Division

Army Form C. 2118.

Place	Date	Hour	Summary of Events and Information	Remarks and references to Appendices
Field	1.11.17		Routine work	R.C.M.
"	2.11.17		Routine work	RCM
"	3.11.17		Routine work	RCM
"	4.11.17		Routine work	RCM
"	5.11.17		Routine work	RCM
"	6.11.17		Routine work	RCM
"	7.11.17		Routine work	RCM
"	8.11.17		Routine work	RCM
"	9.11.17		Routine work	RCM
"	10.11.17		Routine work	RCM
"	11.11.17		Routine work	RCM
"	12.11.17		Routine work	RCM
"	13.11.17		Routine work	RCM
"	14.11.17		Routine work. Capt SCOTT LITTLE AVC joined Division	RCM
"	15.11.17		Went 22 Vety Hosp. for microscopical examination	RCM
"	16.11.17		Routine work. Capt FLYNN AVC leaves division tomorrow	RCM

Army Form C. 2118.

D.A.D.V.S.
31st DIVISION.

No. _____ Date _____

WAR DIARY
or
INTELLIGENCE SUMMARY.
(Erase heading not required.)

DADVS 31st Division

Instructions regarding War Diaries and Intelligence Summaries are contained in F. S. Regs., Part II, and the Staff Manual respectively. Title pages will be prepared in manuscript.

Place	Date	Hour	Summary of Events and Information	Remarks and references to Appendices
Field	17.11.17		Routine work	ACM
"	18.11.17		Routine work	ACM
"	19.11.17		Routine work	ACM
"	20.11.17		Routine work	ACM
"	21.11.17		Routine work	ACM
"	22.11.17		Routine work	ACM
"	23.11.17		Routine work	ACM
"	24.11.17		Routine work	ACM
"	25.11.17		Routine work	ACM
"	26.11.17		Routine work	ACM
"	27.11.17		Routine work	ACM
"	28.11.17		Routine work	ACM
"	29.11.17		Routine work	ACM
"	30.11.17		Routine work	ACM

AC Matthew Major
DADVS 31st Division

Confidential

Volume XXIV

War Diary.

D.A.D.V.S.   31st Division

December 1917.

Army Form C. 2118.

WAR DIARY
or
INTELLIGENCE SUMMARY.

(Erase heading not required.)

DADVS 31st Division

Instructions regarding War Diaries and Intelligence Summaries are contained in F. S. Regs., Part II. and the Staff Manual respectively. Title pages will be prepared in manuscript.

D.A.D.V.S.
31st DIVISION.

Place	Date	Hour	Summary of Events and Information	Remarks and references to Appendices
Field	1.12.17		Routine work	RCM
"	2.12.17		Routine work	RCM
"	3.12.17		Routine work	RCM
"	4.12.17		Routine work	RCM
"	5.12.17		Routine work	RCM
"	6.12.17		Routine work	RCM
"	7.12.17		Routine work	RCM
"	8.12.17		Routine work	RCM
"	9.12.17		Routine work	RCM
"	10.12.17		Routine work	RCM
"	11.12.17		Routine work	RCM
"	12.12.17		Routine work	RCM
"	13.12.17		Routine work	RCM
"	14.12.17		Routine work	RCM
"	15.12.17		Routine work	RCM
"	16.12.17		Routine work	RCM

WAR DIARY *or* INTELLIGENCE SUMMARY.

(Erase heading not required.) DADVS, 31st Division

Army Form C. 2118.

Instructions regarding War Diaries and Intelligence Summaries are contained in F. S. Regs., Part II. and the Staff Manual respectively. Title pages will be prepared in manuscript.

Place	Date	Hour	Summary of Events and Information	Remarks and references to Appendices
Field	17.12.17		Routine work	RCM
"	18.12.17		Routine work	RCM
"	19.12.17		Routine work	RCM
"	20.12.17		Routine work	RCM
"	21.12.17		Routine work	RCM
"	22.12.17		Routine work	RCM
"	23.12.17		Routine work	RCM
"	24.12.17		Routine work	RCM
"	25.12.17		Routine work	RCM
"	26.12.17		Routine work	RCM
"	27.12.17		Routine work	RCM
"	28.12.17		Routine work	RCM
"	29.12.17		Routine work	RCM
"	30.12.17		Routine work	RCM
"	31.12.17		Routine work	RCM

RCMatthews Major
DADVS 31st Division

Army Form C. 2118.

WAR DIARY
or
INTELLIGENCE SUMMARY.
(Erase heading not required.)

DADVS 31st Division Vol 23

D.A.D.V.S. 31st DIVISION.

Place	Date	Hour	Summary of Events and Information	Remarks and references to Appendices
FIELD	1.1.18		Routine work	RCM
"	2.1.18		Two remounts that arrived last night from 4th Reinforced Depot sent down on inspection this morning to have PSOROPTIC MANGE	RCM
"	3.1.18		Routine work	RCM
"	4.1.18		Routine work	RCM
"	5.1.18		Routine work	RCM
"	6.1.18		Capt. G.H. BUTCHER A.V.C. assumed duties of D.A.D.V.S. Maj. Matthews D.S.O. proceeded on leave to England for 14 days.	
"	7-1-18		Routine work	
"	8-1-18		Routine work	
"	9-1-18		Routine work	
"	10-1-18		Routine work	
"	11-1-18		Routine work	
"	12-1-18		Routine work — 1 horse issued to 15th W. York rec'd from 113 F.A. on 10-1-18	
"	13-1-18		Routine work — 1 Horse Casualty from Mange	
"	14-1-18		Routine work	

WAR DIARY or INTELLIGENCE SUMMARY.

(Erase heading not required.)

D.A.D.V.S. 31st Div.

Army Form C. 2118.

D.A.D.V.S.
31st DIVISION.

Place	Date	Hour	Summary of Events and Information	Remarks and references to Appendices
Field	15-1-18		Routine work	GHM
"	16-1-18		Routine work	GHM
"	17-1-18		Routine work	GHM
"	18-1-18		Routine work	GHM
"	19-1-18		Routine work	GHM
"	20-1-18		Routine work	GHM
"	21-1-18		57 Remounts arrived last night from No 4 Base Remount Depot Boulogne – they were inspected today by me & 3 animals were found to be suspicious of Mange & were sent to the M.V.S. Serapys failed to reveal any parasites – necessary precautions have been taken	
"	22-1-18		Routine work	GHM
"	23.1.18		Major A.C. MATTHEWS. AVC assumed duties of DADVS	GHM
"	24.1.18		Routine work	ACM
"	25.1.18		Routine work	ACM
"	26.1.18		Routine work	ACM

Army Form C. 2118.

WAR DIARY
or
INTELLIGENCE SUMMARY.

(Erase heading not required.)

DADVS. 31st Division

Place	Date	Hour	Summary of Events and Information	Remarks and references to Appendices
Field	27.1.18		Routine work	RCM
"	28.1.18		Routine work	RCM
"	29.1.18		Routine work	RCM
"	30.1.18		Routine work	RCM
"	31.1.18		Routine work	RCM

RC Matthew Major AVC
D.A.D.V.S. 31st Division

D.A.D.V.S.
31st DIVISION.

WAR DIARY
or
INTELLIGENCE SUMMARY.
(Erase heading not required.)

Army Form C. 2118.

DADVS 31st Division

D.A.D.V.3.
31st DIVISION

Instructions regarding War Diaries and Intelligence Summaries are contained in F. S. Regs., Part II. and the Staff Manual respectively. Title pages will be prepared in manuscript.

Place	Date	Hour	Summary of Events and Information	Remarks and references to Appendices
Field	17.2.18		Routine Work	RCM
"	18.2.18		Routine work	RCM
"	19.2.18		Routine work	RCM
"	20.2.18		Routine work	RCM
"	21.2.18		Routine work	RCM
"	22.2.18		Routine work	RCM
"	23.2.18		Routine work	RCM
"	24.2.18		Routine work	RCM
"	25.2.18		Routine work	RCM
"	26.2.18		Routine work	RCM
"	27.2.18		Routine work	RCM
"	28.2.18		Routine work	RCM

AC McMahon MRCVS AVC
DADVS 31st Division

Army Form C. 2118.

WAR DIARY
or
INTELLIGENCE SUMMARY.

(Erase heading not required.)

D.A.D.V.S. 31st Division

Vol 24

D.A.D.V.S.
31st DIVISION.
No ....
Date ....

Instructions regarding War Diaries and Intelligence Summaries are contained in F. S. Regs., Part II. and the Staff Manual respectively. Title pages will be prepared in manuscript.

Place	Date	Hour	Summary of Events and Information	Remarks and references to Appendices
Field	1.2.18		Routine work	RCM
"	2.2.18		Routine work	RCM
"	3.2.18		Routine work	RCM
"	4.2.18		Routine work	RCM
"	5.2.18		Routine work	RCM
"	6.2.18		Routine work	RCM
"	7.2.18		Routine work	RCM
"	8.2.18		Routine work	RCM
"	9.2.18		Routine work	RCM
"	10.2.18		Routine work	RCM
"	11.2.18		Routine work	RCM
"	12.2.18		Routine work	RCM
"	13.2.18		Routine work	RCM
"	14.2.18		Routine work	RCM
"	15.2.18		Routine work	RCM
"	16.2.18		Routine work	RCM

Army Form C. 2118.

WAR DIARY
or
INTELLIGENCE SUMMARY.
(Erase heading not required.) D.A.D.V.S. 17 Sept 3/o4 5 Division

Instructions regarding War Diaries and Intelligence Summaries are contained in F.S. Regs., Part II. and the Staff Manual respectively. Title pages will be prepared in manuscript.

D.A.D.V.S.,
31st DIVISION.

Vol 25

Place	Date	Hour	Summary of Events and Information	Remarks and references to Appendices
Field	1.3.18		Routine work	RCM
"	2.3.18		Routine work	RCM
"	3.3.18		Routine work	RCM
"	4.3.18		Move to MIN GOYAL	RCM
"	5.3.18		Routine work	RCM
"	6.3.18		Routine work	RCM
"	7.3.18		Routine work	RCM
"	8.3.18		Routine work	RCM
"	9.3.18		Routine work	RCM
"	10.3.18		Routine work	RCM
"	11.3.18		Routine work	RCM
"	12.3.18		Routine work	RCM
"	13.3.18		Routine work	RCM
"	14.3.18		Attended conference at office of ADVS XIII Corps	RCM
"	15.3.18		Routine work	RCM
"	16.3.18		Routine work	RCM

Army Form C. 2118.

WAR DIARY
or
INTELLIGENCE SUMMARY.
(Erase heading not required.)

DADVS 31st Division

Instructions regarding War Diaries and Intelligence Summaries are contained in F. S. Regs., Part II. and the Staff Manual respectively. Title pages will be prepared in manuscript.

D.A.D.V.S.
31st DIVISION

Place	Date	Hour	Summary of Events and Information	Remarks and references to Appendices
Field	17.3.18		Routine work	RCM
"	18.3.18		Routine work	RCM
"	19.3.18		Routine work	RCM
"	20.3.18		Routine work	RCM
"	21.3.18		Routine work. The 31st Division arrived in France 7th March 1916. For information of officer i/c Records A.V.C. WOOLWICH	RCM
"	22.3.18		Moved to BASSEAUX BASSEUX	RCM
"	23.3.18		Routine work	RCM
"	24.3.18		Routine work	RCM
"	25.3.18		Moved to HUMBERCAMP	RCM
"	26.3.18		Routine work	RCM
"	27.3.18		Routine work	RCM
"	28.3.18		Routine work	RCM
"	29.3.18		Routine work	RCM
"	30.3.18		Routine work	RCM
"	31.3.18		Routine work	RCM

R C Matthews Major
DADVS 31st Division

Army Form C. 2118.

WAR DIARY
or
INTELLIGENCE SUMMARY.
(Erase heading not required.)

D.A.D.V.S. 31st DIVISION

DADVS 31st Division

Place	Date	Hour	Summary of Events and Information	Remarks and references to Appendices
Field	1.4.16		Moved to LUCHEUX	ACM
"	2.4.16		Moved to MINGOVAL	ACM
"	3.4.16		Routine work	ACM
"	4.4.16		Routine work	ACM
"	5.4.16		Routine work	ACM
"	6.4.16		Routine work	ACM
"	7.4.16		Routine work	ACM
"	8.4.16		Routine work	ACM
"	9.4.16		Routine work	ACM
"	10.4.16		Moved to STRAZEELE	ACM
"	11.4.16		Railway work Moved to LE TIR ANGLAIS	ACM
"	12.4.16		Moved to WALLON CAPPEL	ACM
"	13.4.16		Division mobilized 15th June 1915. Joined 31st July 1915. Division proceeded overseas on various dates between 7th Dec 1915 & 14th Jan 1916. Landed on 10th Dec 1915. For information of officers & AVC Records	ACM
"	14.4.16		Routine work	ACM

WAR DIARY
or
INTELLIGENCE SUMMARY.

(Erase heading not required.) DADVS 31st Division

Army Form C. 2118.

DADVS.
31st DIVISION.

Place	Date	Hour	Summary of Events and Information	Remarks and references to Appendices
Field	15.4.18		Routine work	RCM
	16.4.18		Routine work. Moved to STAPLE	RCM
	17.4.18		Routine work	RCM
"	18.4.18		Routine work	RCM
	19.4.18		Routine work	RCM
	20.4.18		Routine work	RCM
	21.4.18		Moved to RACQUINGHEM	RCM
"	22.4.18		Routine work	RCM
"	23.4.18		Routine work	RCM
"	24.4.18		Routine work	RCM
"	25.4.18		Routine work	RCM
"	26.4.18		Routine work	RCM
"	27.4.18		Routine work	RCM
"	28.4.18		Moved to HONDEGHEM	RCM
"	29.4.18		Routine work	RCM
"	30.4.18		Routine work	RCM

A C McArthur Major AVC
DADVS 31st Division

Confidential.

Volume XXIX

War Diary.

D.A.D.V.S.
31st Divn.

May, 1918.

No 27.

Army Form C. 2118.

WAR DIARY
or
INTELLIGENCE SUMMARY.
(Erase heading not required.)

DADVS 31st Division

D.A.D.V.S., 31st DIVISION

Instructions regarding War Diaries and Intelligence Summaries are contained in F. S. Regs., Part II. and the Staff Manual respectively. Title pages will be prepared in manuscript.

Place	Date	Hour	Summary of Events and Information	Remarks and references to Appendices
Field	1.5.18		Routine work	ACM
"	2.5.18		Routine work	ACM
"	3.5.18		Routine work	ACM
"	4.5.18		Routine work	ACM
"	5.5.18		Routine work	ACM
"	6.5.18		Routine work	ACM
"	7.5.18		Routine work	ACM
"	8.5.18		Routine work	ACM
"	9.5.18		Routine work	ACM
"	10.5.18		Routine work	ACM
"	11.5.18		Routine work	ACM
"	12.5.18		Routine work	ACM
"	13.5.18		Routine work	ACM
"	14.5.18		Routine work	ACM
"	15.5.18		Routine work	ACM
"	16.5.18		Routine work	ACM

Army Form C. 2118.

WAR DIARY
or
INTELLIGENCE SUMMARY.

(Erase heading not required.)

DADVS 31st Division

Place	Date	Hour	Summary of Events and Information	Remarks and references to Appendices
Field	17.5.18		Routine work	ACM
"	18.5.18		Routine work	ACM
"	19.5.18		Routine work	ACM
"	20.5.18		Guards Bde. left 31st Division	ACM
"	21.5.18		Routine work	ACM
"	22.5.18		Routine work	ACM
"	23.5.18		Routine work	ACM
"	24.5.18		Routine work	ACM
"	25.5.18		Moved to WARDRECQUES	ACM
"	26.5.18		Routine work	ACM
"	27.5.18		Routine work	ACM
"	28.5.18		Routine work	ACM
"	29.5.18		Routine work	ACM
"	30.5.18		Routine work	ACM
"	31.5.18		Routine work	ACM

A. Matthews Major AVC
DADVS 31st Division

WAR DIARY
or
INTELLIGENCE SUMMARY

(Erase heading not required.)

D.A.D.V.S. 31st Division

Army Form C. 2118.

Place	Date	Hour	Summary of Events and Information	Remarks and references to Appendices
Field	1.6.18		General of H.Q. & Daily file opened. Sgt LODGE, A.V.C. reported for duty	ACM
"	2.6.18		Routine work	ACM
"	3.6.18		Routine work	ACM
"	4.6.18		Routine work	ACM
"	5.6.18		Routine work	ACM
"	6.6.18		Routine work	ACM
"	7.6.18		Routine work	ACM
"	8.6.18		Routine work	ACM
"	9.6.18		Routine work	ACM
"	10.6.18		Routine work	ACM
"	11.6.18		Routine work	ACM
"	12.6.18		Routine work	ACM
"	13.6.18		Routine work	ACM
"	14.6.18		Routine work	ACM
"	15.6.18		Routine work	ACM
"	16.6.18		Routine work	ACM

WAR DIARY
or
INTELLIGENCE SUMMARY.
(Erase heading not required.)

Army Form C. 2118.

DADVS 31st Division

D.A.D.V.S.
31st DIVISION

Place	Date	Hour	Summary of Events and Information	Remarks and references to Appendices
Field	17.6.18		Routine work	RCM
"	18.6.18		Routine work	RCM
"	19.6.18		Routine work	RCM
"	20.6.18		Routine work	RCM
"	21.6.18		Routine work	RCM
"	22.6.18		Move to ST LEDGER	RCM
"	23.6.18		Routine work	RCM
"	24.6.18		Routine work	RCM
"	25.6.18		Routine work	RCM
"	26.6.18		Routine work	RCM
"	27.6.18		Routine work	RCM
"	28.6.18		Routine work	RCM
"	29.6.18		Routine work	RCM
"	30.6.18		Routine work	RCM

W Matthews Major
DADVS 31st Division

Army Form C. 2118.

WAR DIARY
or
INTELLIGENCE SUMMARY.
(Erase heading not required.)

D.A.D.V.S. 31st DIVISION. DADVS 31st Division Vol 29

Place	Date	Hour	Summary of Events and Information	Remarks and references to Appendices
Field	1.7.18		Routine work	ACM
"	2.7.18		Routine work	ACM
"	3.7.18		Routine work	ACM
"	4.7.18		Routine work	ACM
"	5.7.18		Routine work	ACM
"	6.7.18		Routine work	ACM
"	7.7.18		Routine work	ACM
"	8.7.18		Routine work	ACM
"	9.7.18		Routine work	ACM
"	10.7.18		Routine work	ACM
"	11.7.18		Routine work	ACM
"	12.7.18		Routine work	ACM
"	13.7.18		Went to WALLON CAPPEL	ACM
"	14.7.18		Routine work	ACM
"	15.7.18		Routine work	ACM

Army Form C. 2118.

WAR DIARY
or
INTELLIGENCE SUMMARY.

D.A.D.V.S.,
31st DIVISION

(Erase heading not required.)

Instructions regarding War Diaries and Intelligence Summaries are contained in F. S. Regs., Part II. and the Staff Manual respectively. Title pages will be prepared in manuscript.

Place	Date	Hour	Summary of Events and Information	Remarks and references to Appendices
Field	16.7.18		Rouen AMR	ACM
"	17.7.18		Rouen MMR	ACM
"	18.7.18		Rouen MMR	ACM
"	19.7.18		Capt G.H. Buckles AVC resumed duties of DADVS during absence of Maj MATTHEWS AVC on 14 days leave to England.	GWB
"	20.7.18		Routine work	GWB
"	21.7.18		Routine work	GWB
"	22.7.18		Routine work	GWB
"	23.7.18		Attended conference of ADVS XVII Corps	GWB
"	24.7.18		Routine work	GWB
"	25.7.18		Routine work	GWB
"	26.7.18		Routine work	GWB
"	27.7.18		Routine work	GWB
"	28.7.18		Routine work	GWB
"	29.7.18		Routine work	GWB
"	30.7.18		Routine work	GWB
"	31.7.18		Routine work	GWB

Lt Col ADVS 31st Div

Army Form C. 2118.

WAR DIARY
or
INTELLIGENCE SUMMARY.
(Erase heading not required.)

D.A.D.V.S. 31st DIVISION

D.A.D.V.S. 31st Division

Instructions regarding War Diaries and Intelligence Summaries are contained in F. S. Regs., Part II. and the Staff Manual respectively. Title pages will be prepared in manuscript.

Place	Date	Hour	Summary of Events and Information	Remarks and references to Appendices
In Field	1-8-18		Routine work	VR30
"	2-8-18		Routine work	
"	3.8.18		Major MATTHEWS AVC returned from leave & assumed duty	RCM
"	4.8.18		Routine work	RCM
"	5.8.18		Routine work	RCM
"	6.8.18		Routine work	RCM
"	7.8.18		Routine work	RCM
"	8.8.18		Routine work	RCM
"	9.8.18		Routine work	RCM
"	10.8.18		Routine work	RCM
"	11.8.18		Routine work	RCM
"	12.8.18		Routine work	RCM
"	13.8.18		Routine work	RCM
"	14.8.18		Routine work	RCM
"	15.8.18		Routine work	RCM
"	16.8.18		Routine work	RCM

Army Form C. 2118.

WAR DIARY
or
INTELLIGENCE SUMMARY.
(Erase heading not required.)

D.A.D.V.S., 31st Division

Instructions regarding War Diaries and Intelligence Summaries are contained in F. S. Regs., Part II. and the Staff Manual respectively. Title pages will be prepared in manuscript.

Place	Date	Hour	Summary of Events and Information	Remarks and references to Appendices
Field	17.8.18		Routine work	ACM
"	18.8.18		Routine work	ACM
"	19.8.18		Routine work	ACM
"	20.8.18		Routine work	ACM
"	21.8.18		Routine work	ACM
"	22.8.18		Routine work	ACM
"	23.8.18		Routine work	ACM
"	24.8.18		Routine work	ACM
"	25.8.18		Moved to HUNDEGEM HONDEGHEM	ACM
"	26.8.18		Routine work	ACM
"	27.8.18		Routine work	ACM
"	28.8.18		Routine work	ACM
"	29.8.18		Routine work	ACM
"	30.8.18		Routine work	ACM
"	31.8.18		Routine work	ACM

A.M. Matthews Major
D.A.D.V.S.
31st Division

WAR DIARY
or
INTELLIGENCE SUMMARY.
(Erase heading not required.)

Army Form C. 2118.

DADVS 31st Division

Place	Date	Hour	Summary of Events and Information	Remarks and references to Appendices
Full	1.9.18		Routine work	RCM
"	2.9.18		Routine work	RCM
"	3.9.18		Move to near CAESTRE	RCM
"	4.9.18		Routine work	RCM
"	5.9.18		Move to FLETRE	RCM
"	6.9.18		Routine work	RCM
"	7.9.18		Routine work	RCM
"	8.9.18		Routine work	RCM
"	9.9.18		Routine work	RCM
"	10.9.18		Routine work	RCM
"	11.9.18		Routine work	RCM
"	12.9.18		Routine work	RCM
"	13.9.18		Routine work	RCM
"	14.9.18		Routine work	RCM
"	15.9.18		Routine work	RCM
"	16.9.18		Routine work	RCM
"	17.9.18		Routine work	RCM

WAR DIARY
or
INTELLIGENCE SUMMARY

(Erase heading not required.)

DADVS 31st Division

Army Form C. 2118

Instructions regarding War Diaries and Intelligence Summaries are contained in F.S. Regs., Part II. and the Staff Manual respectively. Title Pages will be prepared in manuscript.

D.A.D.V.S.
31st Division

Place	Date	Hour	Summary of Events and Information	Remarks and references to Appendices
Field	18.9.15		Routine work	ACM
"	19.9.15		Routine work	ACM
"	20.9.15		Routine work	ACM
"	21.9.15		Routine work	ACM
"	22.9.15		Routine work	ACM
"	23.9.15		Routine work	ACM
"	24.9.15		Routine work	ACM
"	25.9.15		Routine work	ACM
"	26.9.15		Routine work	ACM
"	27.9.15		Routine work	ACM
"	28.9.15		Routine work	ACM
"	29.9.15		Routine work	ACM
"	30.9.15		Routine work	ACM

R. Matthew Major
DADVS 31st Division

Army Form C. 2118.

WAR DIARY
or
INTELLIGENCE SUMMARY.
(Erase heading not required.)

D.A.D.V.S. 31st Division No. 33

Instructions regarding War Diaries and Intelligence Summaries are contained in F. S. Regs., Part II. and the Staff Manual respectively. Title pages will be prepared in manuscript.

Place	Date	Hour	Summary of Events and Information	Remarks and references to Appendices
Field	1.10.18		Routine work	ACM
"	2.10.18		Routine work	ACM
"	3.10.18		Routine work	ACM
"	4.10.18		Routine work	ACM
"	5.10.18		Routine work	ACM
"	6.10.18		Routine work	ACM
"	7.10.18		Routine work	ACM
"	8.10.18		Routine work	ACM
"	9.10.18		Routine work	ACM
"	10.10.18		Routine work	ACM
"	11.10.18		Routine work	ACM
"	12.10.18		Moved to GOUGH House	ACM
"	13.10.18		Routine work	ACM
"	14.10.18		Routine work	ACM
"	15.10.18		Routine work	ACM
"	16.10.18		Routine work	ACM

Army Form C. 2118.

WAR DIARY
or
INTELLIGENCE SUMMARY.
(Erase heading not required.)

DADVS 31st Division

Instructions regarding War Diaries and Intelligence Summaries are contained in F. S. Regs., Part II. and the Staff Manual respectively. Title pages will be prepared in manuscript.

D.A.D.V.S.
31st DIVISION

Place	Date	Hour	Summary of Events and Information	Remarks and references to Appendices
Field	17.10.18		Routine work	RCM
"	18.10.18		Routine work	RCM
"	19.10.18		Routine work	RCM
"	20.10.18		Moved to CROIX BLANCHE	RCM
"	21.10.18		Moved to LANNOY	RCM
"	22.10.18		Routine work	RCM
"	23.10.18		Routine work	RCM
"	24.10.18		Routine work	RCM
"	25.10.18		Routine work	RCM
"	26.10.18		Routine work	RCM
"	27.10.18		Moved to SANZRAH COURTRAI	RCM
"	28.10.18		Routine work	RCM
"	29.10.18		Routine work	RCM
"	30.10.18		Routine work	RCM
"	31.10.18		Routine work	RCM

RC Matthews Major
DADVS 31st Division

Army Form C. 2118.

WAR DIARY
or
INTELLIGENCE SUMMARY.

(Erase heading not required.)

PADS 31st Division No. 3

Place	Date	Hour	Summary of Events and Information	Remarks and references to Appendices
Field	1.11.18		Action ASSM	RCM
"	2.11.18		Action "	RCM
"	3.11.18		Moved to RENLO	RCM
"	4.11.18		Action ASSM	RCM
"	5.11.18		Action ASSM	RCM
"	6.11.18		Action ASSM	RCM
"	7.11.18		Action ASSM	RCM
"	8.11.18		Action ASSM	RCM
"	9.11.18		Action ASSM	RCM
"	10.11.18		Moved to SWEVEGHEM	RCM
"	11.11.18		Moved to RUYEN	RCM
"	12.11.18		Moved to RENAIX	RCM
"	13.11.18		Found that the Hirt the the men for behind. Bivouacked on the road.	RCM
"			Men attended by officers	
"	14.11.18		Action ASSM	RCM
"			Action ASSM	RCM
"	15.11.18		Lorry containing officer kicked down on road. Moved to POTTELBERG	RCM
"	16.11.18		50% men arrived	RCM
"	17.11.18		Lorry arrived. Ready for 15th 16th 17th written up today	RCM

Army Form C. 2118.

WAR DIARY
or
INTELLIGENCE SUMMARY.
(Erase heading not required.)

A.D.V.S. 31st Division

Place	Date	Hour	Summary of Events and Information	Remarks and references to Appendices
	18.11.18		Renescure	ACM
	19.11.18		Roellen south	ACM
	20.11.18		Roellen north	ACM
	21.11.18		Roellen south	ACM
	22.11.18		Roellen north	ACM
	23.11.18		Roellen north	ACM
	24.11.18		Roellen north	ACM
	25.11.18		Moved to ST OMER	ACM
	26.11.18		Roellen north	ACM
	27.11.18		Roellen north	ACM
	28.11.18		Roellen north	ACM
	29.11.18		Roellen north	ACM
	30.11.18		Roellen south	ACM

R. Matthews Major AVC
A.D.V.S. 31st Division

Army Form C. 2118.

WAR DIARY
or
INTELLIGENCE SUMMARY.
(Erase heading not required.)

PADYS 31st Division

No. S/458
Date 1/14

VO 35

Instructions regarding War Diaries and Intelligence Summaries are contained in F. S. Regs., Part II. and the Staff Manual respectively. Title pages will be prepared in manuscript.

Place	Date	Hour	Summary of Events and Information	Remarks and references to Appendices
Field	1.12.18		Routine work	RCM
"	2.12.18		Routine work	RCM
"	3.12.18		Routine work	RCM
"	4.12.18		Routine work	RCM
"	5.12.18		Routine work	RCM
"	6.12.18		Routine work	RCM
"	7.12.18		Routine work	RCM
"	8.12.18		Routine work	RCM
"	9.12.18		Routine work	RCM
"	10.12.18		Routine work	RCM
"	11.12.18		Routine work	RCM
"	12.12.18		Routine work	RCM
"	13.12.18		Routine work	RCM
"	14.12.18		Routine work	RCM
"	15.12.18		Routine work	RCM
"	16.12.18		Routine work	RCM

Army Form C. 2118.

WAR DIARY
or
INTELLIGENCE SUMMARY.
(Erase heading not required.)

D.A.D.V.S. 1st DIVISION

of D.A.D.V.S. 31st Division

Instructions regarding War Diaries and Intelligence Summaries are contained in F. S. Regs., Part II. and the Staff Manual respectively. Title pages will be prepared in manuscript.

Place	Date	Hour	Summary of Events and Information	Remarks and references to Appendices
Field	17.12.16		Routine work	RCM
"	18.12.16		Routine work	RCM
"	19.12.16		Routine work	RCM
"	20.12.16		Routine work	RCM
"	21.12.16		Routine work	RCM
"	22.12.16		Routine work	RCM
"	23.12.16		Routine work	RCM
"	24.12.16		Routine work	RCM
"	25.12.16		Xmas Day. No work except to attend to horses	RCM
"	26.12.16		Routine work	RCM
"	27.12.16		Routine work	RCM
"	28.12.16		Routine work	RCM
"	29.12.16		Routine work	RCM
"	30.12.16		Routine work	RCM
"	31.12.16		Classification of animals for demonstration taken	RCM

A.McLeeham Major
DADVS 31st Division

Army Form C. 2118.

WAR DIARY
or
INTELLIGENCE SUMMARY.

(Erase heading not required.)

Army Book 3rd Division Vol 36

Instructions regarding War Diaries and Intelligence Summaries are contained in F.S. Regs., Part II. and the Staff Manual respectively. Title pages will be prepared in manuscript.

SIG. SECTION 6/526 1.2.19

Place	Date	Hour	Summary of Events and Information	Remarks and references to Appendices
	1/1/19		Routine work	ACM
	2/1/19		Routine work	ACM
	3/1/19		Routine work	ACM
	4/1/19		Routine work	ACM
	5/1/19		Routine work	ACM
	6/1/19		Routine work	ACM
	7/1/19		Routine work	ACM
	8/1/19		Routine work	ACM
	9/1/19		Routine work	ACM
	10/1/19		Routine work	ACM
	11/1/19		Routine work	ACM
	12/1/19		Routine work	ACM
	13/1/19		Routine work	ACM
	14/1/19		Routine work	ACM
	15/1/19		Routine work	ACM
	16/1/19		Routine work	ACM

Army Form C. 2118.

WAR DIARY
or
INTELLIGENCE SUMMARY.
(Erase heading not required.)

DADVS 31st Division

Place	Date	Hour	Summary of Events and Information	Remarks and references to Appendices
Field	17.1.19		Routine work	PLM
"	18.1.19		Routine work	PLM
"	19.1.19		Routine work	PLM
"	20.1.19		Capt. BUTCHER assumed duties of DADVS during absence of Maj. MATHEW on leave	
"	21.1.19		Routine work	
"	22.1.19		Routine work	
"	23.1.19		Routine work	
"	24.1.19		Routine work	
"	25.1.19		Routine work	
"	26.1.19		Routine work	
"	27.1.19		Routine work	
"	28.1.19		Routine work	
"	29.1.19		Routine work	
"	30.1.19		Routine work	
"	31.1.19		Routine work	

Capt for DADVS 31st Division

WAR DIARY or INTELLIGENCE SUMMARY

Army Form C. 2118.

D.A.D.V.S. 31st Divn

Vol 37

Place	Date	Hour	Summary of Events and Information	Remarks and references to Appendices
Field	1-2-19		Routine work	JMM
"	2-2-19		Routine work	JMM
"	3-2-19		Routine work	JMM
"	4-2-19		Routine work	JMM
"	5-2-19		Routine work	JMM
"	6-2-19		Routine work	JMM
"	7-2-19		Routine work	JMM
"	8-2-19		Major Matthews resumed duty from leave & took over	RCM
"	9-2-19		Routine work	RCM
"	10-2-19		Routine work	RCM
"	11-2-19		Routine work	RCM
"	12-2-19		Routine work	RCM
"	13-2-19		Routine work	RCM
"	14-2-19		Routine work	RCM
"	15-2-19		Routine work	RCM
"	16-2-19		Routine work	RCM

Army Form C. 2118.

WAR DIARY
or
INTELLIGENCE SUMMARY.
(Erase heading not required.)

Instructions regarding War Diaries and Intelligence Summaries are contained in F. S. Regs., Part II. and the Staff Manual respectively. Title pages will be prepared in manuscript.

Place	Date	Hour	Summary of Events and Information	Remarks and references to Appendices
Field	17.2.19		Routine work	RCM
"	18.2.19		Routine work	RCM
"	19.2.19		Routine work	RCM
"	20.2.19		Routine work	RCM
"	21.2.19		Routine work	RCM
"	22.2.19		Routine work	RCM
"	23.2.19		Routine work	RCM
"	24.2.19		Routine work	RCM
"	25.2.19		Routine work	RCM
ST OMER	26.2.19		Routine work	RCM
"	27.2.19		Routine work	RCM
"	28.2.19		Routine work	RCM

W Matthews Major
DADVS 31st Division

Army Form C. 2118.

WAR DIARY
or
INTELLIGENCE SUMMARY. D.A.D.V.S., 31st Division.
(Erase heading not required.)

Place	Date	Hour	Summary of Events and Information	Remarks and references to Appendices
ST OMER	1.3.19		Routine work	RCM
"	2.3.19		Routine work	RCM
"	3.3.19		Routine work	RCM
"	4.3.19		Routine work	RCM
"	5.3.19		Routine work	RCM
"	6.3.19		Routine work	RCM
"	7.3.19		Routine work	RCM
"	8.3.19		Routine work	RCM
"	9.3.19		Routine work	RCM
"	10.3.19		Routine work	RCM
"	11.3.19		Routine work	RCM
"	12.3.19		Routine work	RCM
"	13.3.19		Routine work	RCM
"	14.3.19		Routine work	RCM
"	15.3.19		Routine work	RCM
"	16.3.19		Routine work	RCM

WAR DIARY
or
INTELLIGENCE SUMMARY.

(Erase heading not required.)

Army Form C. 2118.

Place	Date	Hour	Summary of Events and Information	Remarks and references to Appendices
STOMER	17.3.19		Routine work	PLM
"	18.3.19		Routine work	PLM
"	19.3.19		Routine work	PLM
"	20.3.19		Routine work	PLM
"	21.3.19		Routine work	PLM
"	22.3.19		Routine work	PLM
"	23.3.19		Routine work	PLM
"	24.3.19		Routine work	PLM
"	25.3.19		Routine work	PLM
"	26.3.19		Routine work	PLM
"	27.3.19		Routine work	PLM
"	28.3.19		Routine work	PLM
"	29.3.19		Routine work	PLM
"	30.3.19		Routine work. Move to BLONDECQUE	PLM
BLONDECQUE	31.3.19			PLM

R L Matthew Major
ADVS 31st Division

WAR DIARY or INTELLIGENCE SUMMARY

Army Form C. 2118.

D.A.D.V.S. 31 Div.

Place	Date	Hour	Summary of Events and Information	Remarks and references to Appendices
BLENDECQUES	1.4.19		Routine work	RCM
"	2.4.19		Routine work	RCM
"	3.4.19		Routine work	RCM
"	4.4.19		Routine work	RCM
"	5.4.19		Routine work	RCM
"	6.4.19		Routine work	RCM
"	7.4.19		Routine work	RCM
"	8.4.19		Capt. T.D. Taylor RAVC T.F. assumed duties A/DADVS 31st Division vice Major R.E. Matthews WSO leave to command	
"	9.4.19		hq 2 Veterinary Hospital Hare	P.L.Y
"	10.4.19		Routine work	P.L.Y
"	11.4.19		Routine work	P.L.Y
"	12.4.19		Routine work	P.L.Y
"	13.4.19		Routine work	P.L.Y

Army Form C. 2118.

WAR DIARY
or
INTELLIGENCE SUMMARY.
(Erase heading not required.)

D.A.D.V.S. 31st Division.

Place	Date	Hour	Summary of Events and Information	Remarks and references to Appendices
BLENDECQUES	14/4/19		Routine	
"	15/4/19		Routine	
"	16/4/19		Routine	
"	17/4/19		Routine	
"	18/4/19		Routine	
"	19/4/19		Routine. Attending Sale of Horses at St Omer	
"	20/4/19		Routine. Attending Sale of Horses at St Omer	
"	21/4/19		Routine	
"	22/4/19		Routine	
"	23/4/19		Routine	
"	24/4/19		Routine	
"	25/4/19		Routine	
"	26/4/19		Routine	
"	27/4/19		Hqrs A.D.V.S. 31st Division closed at 15 hours. All Records closed.	

Jno. L. Taylor, Capt. R.A.V.C.
A/D.A.D.V.S.
31st Division.

www.ingramcontent.com/pod-product-compliance
Lightning Source LLC
Chambersburg PA
CBHW081436160426
43193CB00013B/2301